Plastics

Ashley Lee

Explore other books at:
WWW.ENGAGEBOOKS.COM

VANCOUVER, B.C.

e→ WWW.ENGAGEBOOKS.COM

Plastics: Level 2
I Can Help Save Earth!
Lee, Ashley 1995 –
Copyright © 2021 Engage Books
Design © 2021 Engage Books

Image on page 26 courtesy of 4ocean
Edited by: A.R. Roumanis

Text set in Arial Regular.
Chapter headings set in Arial Black.

FIRST EDITION / FIRST PRINTING

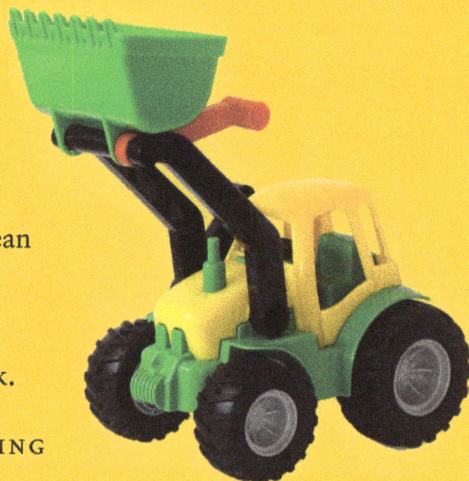

LIBRARY AND ARCHIVES CANADA CATALOGUING IN PUBLICATION

Title: Plastics: I Can Help Save Earth
Names: Lee, Ashley, 1995- author

Identifiers: Canadiana (print) 20200309846 | Canadiana (ebook) 20200309854
ISBN 978-1-77437-712-3 (hardcover)
ISBN 978-1-77437-713-0 (softcover)
ISBN 978-1-77437-714-7 (pdf)
ISBN 978-1-77437-715-4 (epub)
ISBN 978-1-77437-716-1 (audio)

Subjects:
LCSH: Plastic scrap—Environmental aspects—Juvenile literature
LCSH: Plastics—Environmental aspects—Juvenile literature
LCSH: Environmental protection—Citizen participation—Juvenile literature

Classification: LCC TD798 .L44 2020 | DDC J363.72/88—DC23

Contents

What is Plastic?

Plastic is a material that can be made into almost any shape. It can be hard or soft.

Plastic is used to make many different things. It is used in toys, containers, and cars.

How is Plastic Made?

Plastic is made by heating the chemicals in oil, gas, or coal. Oil, gas, and coal all make different kinds of plastic.

There are two main kinds of plastic. Thermoplastics are used in Legos. They can be melted and reshaped many times. Thermosets are used in tires. They can only be melted and shaped once.

Why is Plastic So Popular?

Plastic costs less to make than other materials like metals. It also does not break as easily as other materials like glass.

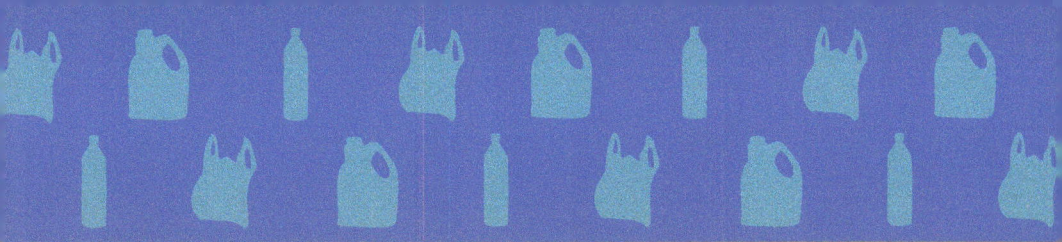

Plastic weighs less than many other materials. This makes it easier to carry and ship across the world.

Plastics Around the World

Plastic products are made all around the world. China, Germany, and the United States create more plastic products than any other countries.

China makes about 60 million tons (61 million metric tons) of plastic every year. The Lego company was started in Denmark. The Great Pacific Garbage Patch is a collection of ocean pollution in the Pacific Ocean. It is about three times larger than France.

Arctic Ocean

Europe

Asia

China

Denmark

Pacific Ocean

Africa

Pacific Ocean

Atlantic Ocean

Australia

0   2,000 miles

0   4,000 kilometers

N

Legend
Land
Ocean

What is Plastic Pollution?

Plastic pollution is when plastic items end up in the **environment**. Some plastics release chemicals into the environment when they are created. This is also a kind of pollution.

KEY WORD

Environment: the surroundings of a person, animal, or plant.

A lot of plastic pollution comes from single-use plastics. These are plastic items that are only used once, like straws or plastic bags. They are thrown away after being used.

Are All Plastics Harmful?

Many plastics are used to make items that help people. Plastics are used in medical equipment, computers, and cell phones.

Single-use plastics create a lot of waste. The average person uses about 540 plastic sandwich bags every year.

Items made out of plastic take more than 400 years to break down.

Plastic Pollution Facts

About 8.6 million tons (8.8 million metric tons) of plastic end up in oceans and rivers every year.

There is around 6.9 billion tons (7 billion metric tons) of plastic waste on Earth.

About 73% of litter found on beaches is plastic.

Around 2 million plastic bags are used around the world every minute.

Scientists believe that more than 90% of all fish and birds have eaten some kind of plastic.

The production of plastic products has doubled in the last 50 years.

How Plastic Pollution Affects Animals

Plastic pollution is found in many animal **habitats**. Animals can get caught in pieces of plastic. They can hurt themselves when they try to break free.

KEY WORD

Habitats: the places where animals live. Different animals live in different habitats.

Some animals try to eat the plastic they find. This can make animals very sick.

How Plastic Pollution Affects Humans

Tiny pieces of plastic called microplastics can end up in human foods. If a person eats an animal that ate plastic, that plastic can end up in the person.

Some plastics have chemicals in them that can enter foods. This is more likely to happen when the plastic is heated. These chemicals can make people very sick.

How Plastic Pollution Affects Earth

Plastic buried in landfills can release chemicals into the ground. These chemicals can end up in water sources.

22

Many countries burn their plastic waste. Burning plastics releases chemicals into the air. These chemicals are one of the causes of **climate change**.

Recycling Plastics

Recycling means turning an old item into something new. Recycled water bottles can be turned into new bottles, containers, or reusable bags.

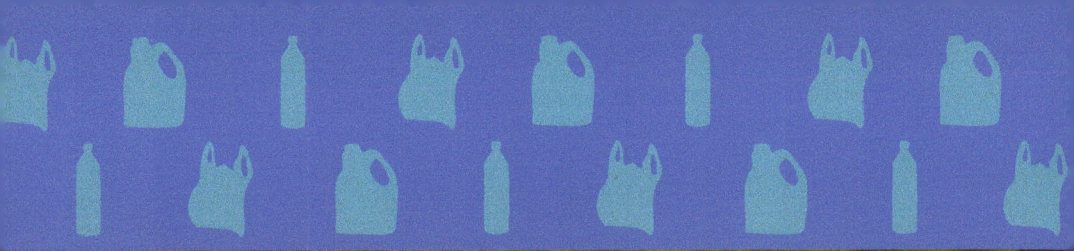

Most kinds of plastic can be taken to a recycling center to be reused. Recycling can help keep plastics out of landfills and animal habitats.

Cleaning Up Plastic Pollution

Some companies are cleaning up plastic from the ocean and recycling it. Recycled plastic can be used to make containers, floor mats, and clothing.

Many people are no longer using single-use plastics. They are finding alternative items they can use over and over again.

Plastic water bottle   **Reusable water bottle**

Sandwich bag   **Container**

Plastic bag   **Cloth bag**

The Future of Plastics

Many countries and cities are banning single-use plastics. This means people can no longer use single-use plastics.

Scientists are working on creating plastics from plant-based materials like sugar and vegetable oil. These plastics would break down faster than other plastics.

YES FOR ECO

100% COMPOSTABLE

Quiz

Test your knowledge of plastics by answering the following questions. The questions are based on what you have read in this book. The answers are listed on the bottom of the next page.

1 How is plastic made?

2 Where was the Lego company started?

3 What are single-use plastics?

4 How long do items made out of plastic take to break down?

5 What does recycling mean?

6 What materials are scientists creating plastics from?

Explore other level 2 readers.

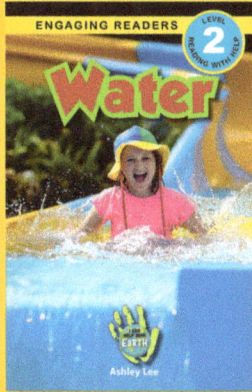

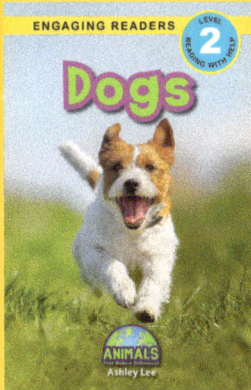

Energy

Food

Goods

Plastics

Water

Butterflies

Dogs

Frogs

Primates

Visit www.engagebooks.com to explore more Engaging Readers.

Answers:
1. By heating the chemicals in oil, gas, or coal 2. Denmark
3. Plastic items that are only used once 4. More than 400 years
5. Turning an old item into something new. 6. Plant-based
materials like sugar and vegetable oil

www.ingramcontent.com/pod-product-compliance
Lightning Source LLC
Chambersburg PA
CBHW051239020426
42331CB00016B/3444